SCIENCE PROJECTS

Matter and Energy

Patricia Whitehouse

Heinemann

www.heinemann.co.uk/library
Visit our website to find out more information about Heinemann Library books.

To order:
☎ Phone 44 (0)1865 888066
🖹 Send a fax to 44 (0)1865 314091
🖥 Visit the Heinemann Library Bookshop at www.heinemann.co.uk/library to browse our catalogue and order online.

First published in Great Britain by Heinemann Library, Halley Court, Jordan Hill, Oxford OX2 8EJ, part of Pearson Education. Heinemann Library is a registered trademark of Pearson Education Ltd.

Produced for Pearson Education by White-Thomson Publishing Ltd. Bridgewater Business Centre, 210 High Street, Lewes, East Sussex BN7 2NH

Editorial: Harriet Brown
Design: Tim Mayer and Alison Walper
Illustrations: Cavedweller Studio
Picture research: Amy Sparks
Production: Duncan Gilbert

Originated by Modern Age
Printed and bound in China by Leo Paper Group

ISBN 978 0 431 04041 7 (hardback)
12 11 10 09 08
10 9 8 7 6 5 4 3 2 1

ISBN 978 0 431 04048 6 (paperback)
12 11 10 09 08
10 9 8 7 6 5 4 3 2 1

British Library Cataloguing in Publication Data
Whitehouse, Patricia, 1958-
Matter. – (Science projects)
530
A full catalogue record for this book is available from the British Library.

Acknowledgements
The author and publishers are grateful to the following for permission to reproduce copyright material: Martyn Chillmaid, **pp. 6, 14, 29, 34, 42**; Corbis/Reinhard Eisele/zefa, **p. 32**; Ecoscene/Eric Needham, **p. 24**; Istockphoto.com, **title page** (Moritz von Hacht), **pp. 8** (Tan Kian Khoon), **16** (Duncan Walker), **20** (Holly Kuchera), **28** (Gianluca Camporesi), **36** (Jacob Yuri Wackerhausen); Masterfile/Andrew Douglas, **p. 4**; Photolibrary/Gay Garry, **p. 12**; Science Photo Library/Peter Menzel, **p. 40**

Cover photograph reproduced with permission of Josh Westrich/Photolibrary

The publishers would like to thank Sue Glass for her assistance in the preparation of this book.

Every effort has been made to contact copyright holders of any material reproduced in this book. Any omissions will be rectified in subsequent printings if notice is given to the publishers.

Contents

» Any words appearing in bold, **like this,** are explained in the glossary.

Starting your science investigation

A science investigation is an exciting challenge. It starts with an idea that you can test by doing experiments. These are often lots of fun to do. But it is no good just charging in without planning first. A good scientist knows that they must first research their idea thoroughly, work out how they can test it, and plan their experiments carefully. When they have done these things, they can happily carry out their experiments to see if their idea is right.

Your experiments might support your original idea or they might shoot it down in flames. This doesn't matter. The important thing is that you will have found out a bit more about the world around you, and had fun along the way. You will be a happy scientist!

In this book, you'll look at nine science investigations involving matter and energy. You'll be able to discover some wonderful things about the world you live in.

Do your research

Is there something about matter and energy you've always wondered about? Something you don't quite understand but would like to? Then do a little research about the subject. Go to the library and find some books about the subject. Books written for students are often a very good place to start.

Use your favourite Internet search engine to find reliable online resources. Websites written by museums, universities, newspapers, and scientific journals are among the best sources for **accurate** research. Each investigation in this book has some suggestions for further research.

You need to make sure that your resources are reliable when doing research. Ask yourself the following questions, especially about the resources you find online.

The investigations

Background information

The start of each investigation contains a box like this.

Possible question

This question is a suggested starting point for your investigation. You will need to adapt the question to suit the things that interest you.

Possible hypothesis

This is only a suggestion. Don't worry if your hypothesis doesn't match the one listed here. Use your imagination!

Approximate cost of materials

Discuss this with your parents before starting work. Don't spend too much.

Materials needed

Make sure you can easily get all of the materials listed and gather them together before starting work.

Level of difficulty

There are three levels of investigations in this book: Easy, Intermediate, and Advanced. The level of difficulty is based on how long the investigation takes and how complicated it is.

1) How old is the resource? Is the information up to date or is it very old?

2) Who wrote the resource? Is the author identified so you know who they are, and what qualifies them to write about the topic?

3) What is the purpose of the resource? A website from a business or pressure group might not give balanced information, but one from a university probably will.

4) Is the information well documented? Can you tell where the author got their information from so you can check how accurate it is?

Some websites allow you to "chat" online with experts. Make sure you discuss this with a parent or teacher first. Never give out personal information online. The "Think U Know" website at http://www.thinkuknow.co.uk has loads of tips about safety online.

Once you know a little more about the subject you want to investigate, you'll be ready to work out your scientific question. You will be able to use this to make a sensible **hypothesis**. A hypothesis is an idea about why something happens that can be tested by doing experiments. Finally, you'll be ready to begin your science investigation!

You can use simple equipment to explore matter and energy in the world around you.

What is an experiment?

Often when someone says that they are going to do an experiment, they mean they are just going to fiddle with something to see what happens. But scientists mean something else. They mean that they are going to control the **variables** involved in a careful way. A variable is something that changes or can be changed. Independent variables are things that you deliberately keep the same or change in your experiment. You should always aim to keep all the independent variables constant, except for the one you are investigating. The dependent variable is the change that happens because of the one independent variable that you do change. You make a fair test if you set up your experiment so that you only change one independent variable at a time. Your results are valid if you have carried out a fair test, and recorded your results or observations honestly.

Sometimes you might want to compare one group with another to see what happens. For example, if you wanted to show the effect of salt on the freezing point of water, you might use 10 cups of water. You would not add salt to five of them (Group A) but you would add salt to the other five cups (Group B). You would put all 10 cups in the freezer. Group A is your **control** group and group B is your test group. You would be looking to see if there is a difference between the two groups. In this experiment, the salt is the independent variable, and the effect on the freezing point is the dependent variable.

You must do experiments carefully so that your results are accurate and reliable. Ideally, you would get the same results if you did your investigation all over again.

Your hypothesis

Once you've decided on the question you're going to try to answer, you then make a scientific **prediction** of what you'll find out in your science project.

For example, if you wonder why you have to get out of the water at the beach when there's lightning, your question might be, "Does water conduct electricity?". Remember, a hypothesis is an idea about why something happens, which can be tested by doing experiments. So your hypothesis in response to the above question might be, "Salt water conducts electricity.". With a hypothesis, you can also work out if you can actually do the experiments needed to answer your question. Think of a question like: "How much electricity is there in the world?". It would be impossible to support your hypothesis, however you express it. This is because you can't possibly measure all of the electricity in the world. So, be sure you can actually get the **evidence** needed to support or disprove your hypothesis.

Keeping records

Good scientists keep careful notes in their lab book about everything they do. This is really important. Other scientists may want to try out the experiments to see if they get the same results. So the records in your lab book need to be clear and easy to follow. What sort of things should you write down?

It is a good idea to write some notes about the research you found in books and on websites. You should also include the names of the books or the web addresses. This will save you from having to find these useful resources all over again later. You should also write down your hypothesis and your reasons for it. All your **data** and results should go into your lab book, too.

Your results are the evidence that you use to make your conclusion. Never rub out an odd-looking result or tweak it to "look right". An odd result may turn out to be important later. You should write down *every* result you get. Tables are a really good way to record lots of results clearly. Make sure you record when you did your experiments, and anything you might have changed along the way to improve them. No detail is too small when it comes to scientific research.

There are tips for making a great report with each investigation and at the end of this book. Use them as guides and don't be afraid to be creative. Make it *your* investigation!

Rainbow temperature

Stand inside a glass greenhouse and you can feel the heat. The clear glass allows the sun's rays through to heat up the air, the ground, and the plants inside. The glass keeps the heated air contained. Sunlight is actually made up of a spectrum of colours. Are the different light colours different temperatures? Can you measure the difference in temperature? Try this experiment if you'd like to find out.

Do your research

You'll need to do this experiment on a very sunny day. Before you begin this project, do some research on greenhouses and the colours that make up sunlight. Once you've done some research, you can tackle this project. Or, you may come up with your own unique project after you've read and learned more about the topic.

You could start your research with this book and these websites:

» *Everyday Science: Seeing Things: Light*, Ann Fullick (Heinemann, 2005)
» Environmental protection agency: The greenhouse effect: http://www.epa.gov/globalwarming/kids/greenhouse.html
» Cool cosmos: Herschel's experiment: http://coolcosmos.ipac.caltech.edu//cosmic_classroom/classroom_activities/herschel_experiment2.html

Background information

Possible question

Does the colour of light affect the temperature of the surrounding air?

Possible hypothesis

Different colours of light produce different temperatures.

Level of difficulty	Approximate cost of materials
Intermediate	£7.00

Materials needed

» Non-toxic black paint
» Paintbrush
» Five alcohol thermometers, small enough to fit in the cups. You may be able to borrow the thermometers from your school science lab.
» Five large clear plastic cups
» Sheets of cellophane or plastic wrap in red, yellow, blue, and clear, large enough to cover the cups
» Clear sticky tape
» Scissors
» A sunny place to do the experiment

Outline of methods

1. Use the black paint to cover the bulbs of all five thermometers, and let them dry. Blackened bulbs absorb heat better than clear bulbs do.

2. Cover four of the cups, each with one of the sheets of cellophane or plastic wrap. Make sure you completely cover the cup without overlapping the cellophane. Use as little tape as possible.

3. Leave the fifth cup uncovered. This will be your control.

Step 1

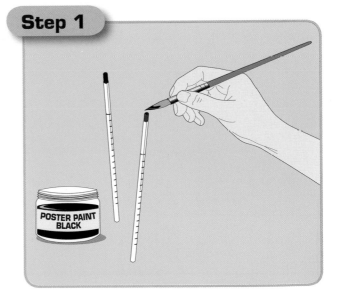

POSTER PAINT BLACK

Continued

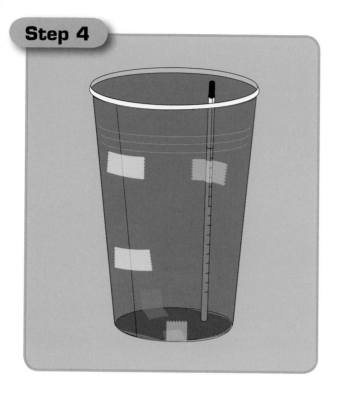

4. Attach a thermometer to the inside of each cup with a loop of tape. The bulb of the thermometer should be near the top of the cup, but should not touch it. Make sure you can read the thermometer without moving the cup.

5. Observe and record the temperature in each cup.

6. Place all five cups in a sunny place. Observe and record the temperature in each cup once every minute for 15 minutes.

Step 6

Analysis of results

» Was there an increase in temperature in the cups?

» Did any of the cups show a higher temperature than the others?

» At what time did you notice a change?

» Can you arrange the cups in order from greatest to smallest temperature change?

More activities to extend your investigation

» Repeat the experiment in the same conditions and average your data. Find the average by adding the temperatures for each minute for each colour; then divide the total temperature by the number of trials. A greater number of trials will increase the accuracy of your results.

» Try using additional colours of cellophane or plastic wrap.

» Extend the time you collect data.

» Try the experiment on a cooler day and see how the change affects the results.

Project extras

» Include pieces of the coloured cellophane in your report to show the exact colours used.

» Take photographs of the experimental set-up and stick these in your report.

» Show your results in both table and graph forms. Choose colours for your graph that match your cup colours.

Warming up to magnets

Magnets produce a magnetic field, which attracts some metals, such as iron and steel. Is the magnetic field changed by the temperature of a magnet? Does cooling or heating a magnet affect its strength? This experiment will help you find out.

Do your research

This project deals with magnetic properties. Before you begin your project, do some research to find out more about ceramic magnets and magnetism. Once you've done some research, you can tackle this project. Or, you may come up with your own unique project after you've read and learned more about the topic.

Here are some books and websites you could start with in your research:

» *Everyday Science: Opposites Attract: Magnetism*, Steve Parker (Heinemann, 2004)
» *Magnet Science*, Glen Vecchione (Sterling, 2006)
» NASA: Information about magnetism: http://www-istp.gsfc.nasa.gov/ Education/Imagnet.html
» Exploratorium: Science snacks about magnetism: http://www.exploratorium .edu/snacks/iconmagnetism.html

Background information

Possible question

Does a ceramic magnet's temperature affect its strength?

Possible hypothesis

Difference in temperature changes the strength of a ceramic magnet.

Level of difficulty	Approximate cost of materials
Easy	£8.00

Materials needed

» An alcohol thermometer or a digital thermometer
» A freezer
» Three ceramic ring magnets
» Six 100-count boxes of medium-sized paper clips
» Plastic tongs
» A heat source, such as a gas ring or hob top
» A metal pan and aluminium foil, or an aluminium or non-metal pan for boiling water, such as one made from borosilicate (Pyrex is a common brand name of this material)
» Water
» Oven gloves
» Adult supervisor

Outline of methods

1. Put the thermometer in the freezer. After 10 minutes, record the temperature.

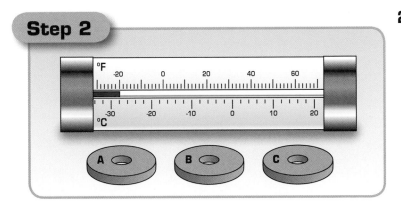

Step 2

2. Label three ceramic magnets A, B, and C. Put them in the freezer near the thermometer. Leave them in the freezer for 10 minutes. Check to see that the temperature remains constant.

Continued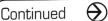

3. Put the three boxes of paper clips into three separate piles on a flat, non-metal surface. Separate any that are hooked together.

4. Remove magnet A from the freezer with the plastic tongs and place it in the middle of the first pile of paper clips. Turn it over with the tongs so that it is covered with paper clips.

Step 4

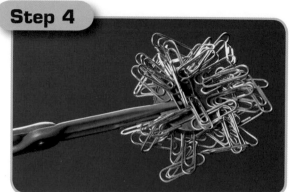

5. Remove the paper clips from the magnet. Count and record the number of paper clips the magnet held.

6. Demagnetise the paper clips by dropping them several times from a height of about 50 centimetres (20 inches) onto a table. Return the paper clips to their original pile.

7. Return the magnet to the freezer for 10 minutes.

8. Repeat steps 4 to 7 two more times with magnet A.

9. Repeat the process with magnets B and C and the two remaining paper clip piles.

10. If you are using a metal pan to boil water, cover the bottom of the pan with several layers of aluminium foil. Then half fill the container with water.

11. Heat the water until it is boiling. Boiling water is 100 °C (212 °F).

ADULT SUPERVISION REQUIRED

12. Put on your oven gloves. Use the tongs to place magnet A in the boiling water and let it boil for 10 minutes.

13. Set up the remaining three boxes of paper clips as in step 3.

14. After 10 minutes, use the tongs to remove the magnet from the boiling water. Repeat the process of attracting, removing, and demagnetising the paper clips as you did in steps 4 to 6. Allow the magnet to cool before you remove the paper clips. Return the magnet to the water for 10 minutes and repeat this step twice more.

Step 12

15. Repeat steps 11 to 14 with magnets B and C.

Analysis of results

» What was the average number of paper clips the cold magnet picked up? To calculate the average, add the number of paper clips picked up in each trial; then divide by the number of trials.

» What was the average number of paper clips the heated magnet picked up?

» Did heating change the magnets' strength?

» What can you infer about the magnetic properties of the materials used for making the magnets?

More activities to extend your investigation

» Increase the number of magnets used – more information increases the accuracy of the results.

» Try the experiment using ceramic magnets at room temperature. Compare the results with those obtained when you heated and cooled the magnets.

» Research other types of materials that are used for making magnets, and use them in your experiment.

» Research the Curie temperature and magnetism.

» Research what might happen to a magnet's strength if you could cool it to a lower temperature using dry ice. Dry ice is solid carbon dioxide. It has a temperature of –78.5 °C (–109.3 °F).

Project extras

» Include photographs of various stages in your experiment.

» Make a graph to show the results of your experiment.

Power in the solution

Electricity flows through materials that are **conductors,** such as copper wire. Wire is a solid. Electricity also flows through some liquids. Liquids that conduct electricity are called **electrolytes.** Electrolytes are usually **solutions.** Is water an electrolyte? Does it conduct electricity? Does adding materials to water cause an electric current to flow through it? You can find out if you try this project.

Do your research

In this experiment, you will need to create an electric **circuit.** Part of the circuit will be the solutions you make. Before you begin this project, do some research on electric circuits and electrolytes. You'll be making solutions from acids, bases, and salts, so do some research on them, too. Make sure you do this experiment in a well-ventilated room—small amounts of chlorine gas may be produced when salt water is used as the electrolyte. Once you've done some research, you can try this project. Or, you may come up with your own unique project after you've read and learned more about the topic.

You could start your research with this book and these websites:

» *Chemicals in Action: Acids and Bases*, Chris Oxlade (Heinemann, 2007)

» Electrolytes: http://dl.clackamas.cc.or.us/ch105-03/electrol.htm

» What is electricity?: http://www.eia.doe.gov/kids/energyfacts/sources/electricity.html

Background information

Possible question

Does a saltwater solution conduct enough electricity to light a torch light bulb?

Possible hypothesis

A saltwater solution is an electrolyte, so it will conduct electricity. Water with more salt in it will conduct better than water with less salt in it.

Level of difficulty

Advanced

Approximate cost of materials:

£11.00

Materials needed

» Two **D batteries** and battery holder with clips
» Torch light bulb in holder with clips
» 250-millilitre (8.5-fluid-ounce) glass beaker or cup
» Coated copper wire
» Wire cutters and wire stripper
» Two carbon **electrodes**
» 100 millilitres (3.4 fluid ounces) tap water
» 100 millilitres (3.4 fluid ounces) distilled water
» 30 grams (2 tablespoons) salt
» 5-millilitre spoon (1 teaspoon)
» A ruler   » Adult supervisor

Outline of methods

1. Build an electric circuit by following these steps:

   a. Put the D batteries in the battery holder. Check that the batteries are facing in the correct directions.

   b. Place the light bulb in the holder; put it near the battery holder.

   c. Put the beaker that will hold the solutions between the battery holder and the light bulb holder.

   d. **Caution: Ask an adult to help you cut and strip the wire.** Measure and cut three lengths of wire; strip the plastic coating from the ends. One wire connects one end of the battery holder to the light bulb holder. A second wire connects the other end of the light bulb holder. The third wire connects to the remaining clip of the battery holder.

ADULT SUPERVISION REQUIRED

Continued

e. One wire coming from the battery and one wire from the light bulb should be long enough to reach into the glass beaker. Tightly coil each end of these wires around an end of each electrode.

2. Touch the electrodes together. The light bulb should light up. If it doesn't, make sure that each wire in the circuit is connected. Also make sure that opposite ends of the batteries are connected.

3. Fill the beaker with 100 millilitres (3.4 fluid ounces) *tap* water.

4. Place the electrodes in the beaker; make sure they are not touching each other. Note: Each time you put the electrodes in the liquid, keep the distance between them the same. Observe and record whether the bulb is lit. Remove the electrodes.

5. Fill the beaker with 100 millilitres (3.4 fluid ounces) *distilled* water.

6. Repeat step 4.

7. Add 5 grams (1 teaspoon) of salt to the beaker and stir. Replace the electrodes and observe the bulb.

8. If the bulb does not light, continue to stir in salt in 1-teaspoon (5-millilitre) increments and see if the bulb will light, until you've added a maximum of 5 teaspoons (25 millilitres). Record your observations.

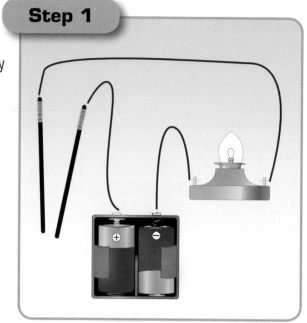

Step 1

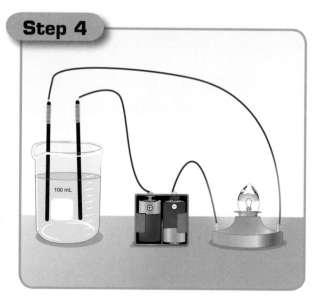

Step 4

100 mL

Analysis of results

» Did plain tap water or distilled water cause the bulb to light?

» Did the salt water cause the bulb to light?

» How much salt did you need to add to light the bulb?

» Did the light intensity vary as you added salt?

» What factors apart from the water's salt content might have affected the results?

More activities to extend your investigation

» Repeat the experiment using fresh batteries and a new light bulb; check your earlier results against this second trial.

» Research the properties of salt and water.

» Add salt to tap water instead of distilled water and report your results.

» Try adding other materials, such as vinegar, baking soda, or cola, to the water.

Project extras

» Include photographs of your experiment. Label each photograph with the amount of salt you used.

» Research electrical symbols. Draw a diagram of your circuit. Where possible draw symbols to represent the components of the circuit.

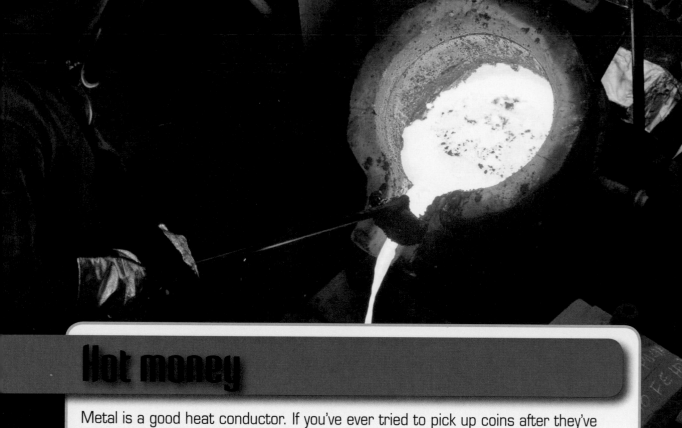

Hot money

Metal is a good heat conductor. If you've ever tried to pick up coins after they've been sitting on the dashboard of a car on a hot, sunny day, you know they can get really hot! But how hot can they get? Does one kind of coin conduct heat better than the others? Try this experiment and find out.

Do your research

This experiment looks at heat conduction. Before you begin this project, do some research on conduction, metals, and **alloys.** You'll also need to know which alloys make up the coins you use in this experiment. Once you've done some research, you can tackle this project. Or, you may come up with your own unique project after you've read and learned more about the topic.

Here are some books and websites you could start with in your research:

» *Physical Science In Depth: Heating and Cooling*, Carol Ballard (Heinemann, 2007)

» *Using Materials: How We Use Metals*, Chris Oxlade (Raintree, 2005)

» UK coin specifications: http://www.royalmint.com/RoyalMint/web/site/Corporate/Corp_british_coinage/CurrentSpecifications.asp

Background information

Possible question

Which coin is the best heat conductor?

Possible hypothesis

A penny is the best heat conductor.

Level of difficulty

Intermediate

Approximate cost of materials

£5.00

Materials needed

» 12 pennies
» 12 two-pence pieces
» 12 five-pence pieces
» 12 twenty-pence pieces
» A ruler
» A griddle or frying pan
» 12 birthday candles
» A hob top
» A stopwatch
» Oven gloves
» Kitchen towel
» Metal tongs   » Adult supervisor

» Cool cosmos: How does heat travel?: http://coolcosmos.ipac.caltech.edu/cosmic_classroom/light_lessons/thermal/transfer.html
» Heat transfer: http://www.bbc.co.uk/schools/gcsebitesize/physics/energy/energytransferrev6.shtml

Outline of methods

1. Make stacks of each type of coin so they are all as close to the same height as you can make them. Use no more than four coins in each stack. Use a ruler to measure the stacks.

Step 1

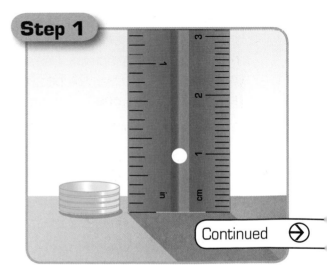

Continued ➔

2. Place each stack of coins the same distance from the centre of the pan. This will ensure that each stack gets an equal amount of heat.

3. Cut a piece 1 centimetre (⅓ inch) long from the bottom of four birthday candles. Place one piece of candle on the top of each stack of coins.

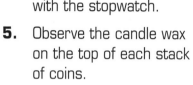

4. Caution: Ask an adult to help you use the hob top. Put the pan on the hob, turn the dial to the lowest temperature setting, and begin timing the experiment with the stopwatch.

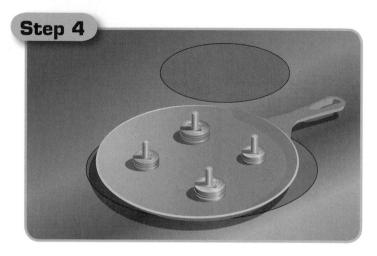

Step 4

5. Observe the candle wax on the top of each stack of coins.

6. Record when the wax begins to melt and when it is completely melted.

7. Turn off the hob when all the wax is completely melted.

8. Caution: The coins and melted wax will be hot. You must use tongs and wear oven gloves for the next part of the experiment. An adult should be present to supervise.
Place kitchen towel over the stacks of coins to absorb some of the melted wax. Use the tongs to remove the stacks of coins from the hob top.

ADULT SUPERVISION REQUIRED

9. Repeat the experiment two more times, using new coins and candle pieces each time. Before you repeat the experiment, you'll need to let the pan and hob top cool to room temperature. You might need to wait a few hours for them to cool, or you might want to do the experiment on two different days. Record and average your results. To average your results, add together how long it took the wax to melt for each type of coin; then divide that number by the number of trials.

Analysis of results

» What was the average time for the wax to begin melting on top of each coin stack?

» What was the average time for the wax to be completely melted on each coin stack?

» Was there a difference in the time it took for each type of coin? If so, which coin stack was fastest?

» What materials were the coins made from? Make sure you check the date of your coins because that may affect their composition.

» What can you infer about the **conductivity** of each metal alloy?

» What other factors might be involved?

More activities to extend your investigation

» Describe the metals used in the coins you tested.

» Research the type of alloys used for coins that were minted in different years. Include in your report the years of minting for all the coins you used.

» Include additional coins in your experiment, such as a one-pound and a two-pound coins.

» See how your results are affected if you use coins from another country.

Project extras

» Show the melt rate in both table and graph forms.

» Draw a table to show which metals are found in each of the coins that you used.

» Photograph your experimental set-up and include the pictures in your report.

Electric attraction

Electromagnets use electricity to create a magnetic field. You probably use electromagnets every day because they are inside appliances, telephones, and speakers. They are also used to move large pieces of metal from one place to another. In this experiment, you will learn how to make an electromagnet. Once you do, can you increase its strength?

Do your research

Before you begin this project, do some research on electricity and magnetism. You'll also need to know how to build an electric circuit. Once you've done some research, you can tackle this project. Or, you may come up with your own unique project after you've read and learned more about the topic.

Here are some books and websites you could start with in your research:

» *Everyday Science: Opposites Attract: Magnetism*, Steve Parker (Heinemann, 2004)

» NASA: How to build an electromagnet: http://ksnn.larc.nasa.gov/videos_cap.cfm?unit=electromagnet

» Electromagnets: http://www.bbc.co.uk/schools/gcsebitesize/physics/electricity_and_magnetism/electromagnetic_forcesrev3.shtml

Background information

Possible question

Does the thickness of wire affect the strength of an electromagnet?

Possible hypothesis

Thicker wires increase an electromagnet's strength.

Level of difficulty

Advanced

Approximate cost of materials

£7.00

Materials needed

» 100-centimetre (40-inch) coated wire, thin **gauge**
» A ruler
» Wire cutters and wire stripper
» A large nail or bolt, at least 10 centimetres (4 inches) long
» Two D batteries
» A D battery holder, with clips on either end
» Three boxes of 100 small metal paper clips
» 100-centimetre (40-inch) coated copper wire, thick gauge
» Adult supervisor

Outline of methods

1. Build an electromagnetic circuit by following these steps:

    ADULT SUPERVISION REQUIRED

    a. **Caution: Ask an adult to help you strip the wire.** Strip about 3 centimetres (1.2 inches) of the plastic covering from both ends of the thin-gauge wire.

    b. Tightly wind the thin-gauge wire around the nail, starting about 15 centimetres (6 inches) from the end of the wire. Begin at the head of the nail and neatly coil the wire around to the pointed end. Do not overlap the wire. Make 30 coils in the wire.

Step 1b

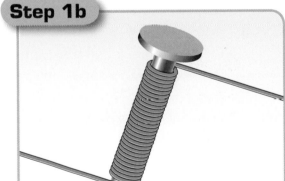

Continued ⊕

c. Put a D battery in the battery holder.

d. Attach one end of the wire to the clip at one end of the holder.

2. Put one box of paper clips onto a non-metallic surface, such as a wooden table-top. Spread out the paper clips a bit and make sure none of them are connected.

3. Attach the other end of the stripped wire to the other clip on the battery holder. Your electromagnet should now be working.

4. Touch the head end of the nail to the pile of paper clips. Lift the nail up and move it away from the pile.

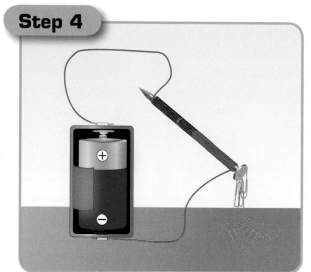

Step 4

5. Disconnect one end of the wire from the battery holder so the electromagnet no longer works. The paper clips should fall from the nail. Count and record the number of paper clips that you lifted. Note: Keep the wire disconnected from the battery holder until you are ready to use it again.

6. Add new paper clips to the pile so there are 100 in the pile. Do not re-use the lifted paper clips because they may have become temporary magnets during the experiment.

7. Reconnect the wire and repeat steps 4 to 6 two more times. Record your results. Take an average of your results by adding the three results together and then dividing by three.

8. Disconnect the thin-gauge wire from the battery holder and uncoil it from the nail. Put a new D battery in the battery holder. Attach the thick-gauge wire to make an electromagnet circuit as you did in step 1.

9. Repeat the procedure you used for the thin-gauge wire electromagnet (steps 2 to 7).

Analysis of results

» What was the average number of paper clips each electromagnet picked up?

» Did one electromagnet pick up more paper clips than the other?

» What other factors besides the thickness of the wire might have affected the results?

More activities to extend your investigation

» Research the history of electromagnets and electromagnetism.

» Research what would happen to an electromagnet's strength if you used a glass rod or an aluminium nail as the core of the electromagnet. If you are able to find the necessary equipment, carry out this alternate investigation. Compare these results with the original results.

Project extras

» Make a graphic that shows everyday items that use electromagnets.

» Research how to draw electric schematic diagrams. Include a diagram of your circuit in your report.

» Draw an accurate diagram of the electromagnets you made, and include information about how electromagnets work.

» Include photos of your electromagnets as part of your report, showing the number of paper clips each electromagnet picked up.

Bright ideas

If you were asked to go to the shops to buy a 60-watt light bulb, you might be surprised at the variety of 60-watt bulbs you had to choose from. Do you need a pearl bulb, a clear bulb, or perhaps a soft-white one? Does each type of bulb give you the same amount of light? Does each give off the same amount of heat? This experiment will help you find out.

Do your research

You will use **incandescent** light bulbs in this experiment. They give off light when electricity causes a thin wire called a filament to heat up so much that it glows. Before you begin, do some research on incandescent light and on **lumens.** A lumen is a unit of measurement of the brightness of light. Once you've done some research, you can shed some light on this project. Or, you may come up with your own unique project after you've read and learned more about the topic.

Background information

Possible question

Do different types of incandescent light bulbs with the same **wattage** release different amounts of heat?

Possible hypothesis

Different types of incandescent light bulbs release different amounts of heat.

Level of difficulty

Easy

Approximate cost of materials

£7.00

Materials needed

» A flexible desk lamp
» A ruler
» An alcohol thermometer
» Sticky tape
» 60-watt light bulbs of various types: pearl, clear, soft white, and reflector
» Oven gloves
» Adult supervisor

Here are some books and websites you could start with in your research:

» *Inventions That Shaped the World: The Light Bulb*, John R Matthews (Franklin Watts, 2005)
» The history of the light bulb: http://invsee.asu.edu/Modules/lightbulb/meathist.htm
» Why does a filament give off light?: http://invsee.asu.edu/Modules/lightbulb/filament.htm
» Maths: Measuring light: http://www.gelighting.com/na/home_lighting/gela/students/math.htm

A light bulb's wattage is usually printed on the bulb.

240V
60W

Continued

Outline of methods

Caution: An adult should be present to help you at all times during this experiment. Do not look directly at the light bulbs when they are on. Wait several minutes after the light has been turned off and the lamp is unplugged before removing the bulb. Use oven gloves when removing the light bulb.

ADULT SUPERVISION REQUIRED

1. Put the flexible desk lamp on a heat-resistant surface, such as a table-top or work surface.

Steps 3 and 4

Step 5

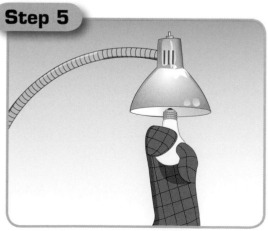

2. Bend the lamp so that the light bulb is no further than 15 centimetres (6 inches) from the table-top.

3. Place a thermometer directly under the part of the lamp that holds the light bulb. Tape the thermometer in place to keep it from moving during the experiment. Wait five minutes and record the temperature at the surface.

4. Put one of the light bulbs in the lamp, plug in the lamp, and turn it on. Record the temperature every five minutes for 30 minutes.

5. After 30 minutes, turn off the lamp and unplug it. Allow the light bulb to cool before you remove it. Use oven gloves when removing the bulb. Allow the thermometer on the table-top to cool to the original temperature.

6. Repeat steps 4 to 5 using the other light bulbs.

Analysis of results

» Was there a difference in the end temperature for any of the light bulbs you tried? If so, what was the difference?

» Can you rank the light bulbs in order of temperature change?

» Did all the light bulbs increase in temperature at the same rate over the 30-minute period?

More activities to extend your investigation

» Increase the number of trials for each light bulb used in this experiment. A greater number of trials will increase the accuracy of your results.

» Look at the lumens ratings on your light bulb packages. Review your experiment results to determine whether the bulbs with higher lumens ratings produced more heat.

» Use light bulbs that are labelled energy efficient. Note the effect on your results.

Project extras

» Include the cardboard containers from your light bulbs in your report.

» Show your results in both table and graph forms.

fun in the sun

When the temperature is in the 20s, you may think it's great to be outside. But did you know that the air temperature around your feet can be completely different, depending on where you're walking? Some surfaces can become very hot, and the air temperature just above those surfaces increases as well. Above which surface will the air temperature change the most? Bring your thermometers and find out.

Do your research

Do this experiment on a warm, sunny day when there is no wind. To get the best results, you'll need to repeat the experiment on at least three days with similar temperatures, so plan your time accordingly. You'll also need quick access to several outdoor surfaces, such as tarmac, concrete, wood, and grass, that remain in sunlight most of the day. Before you begin this project, do some research on the sun and how the sun's heat travels to Earth. Once you've done some research, you can tackle this project. Or, you may come up with your own unique project after you've read and learned more about the topic.

Background information

Possible question

Do different surfaces affect the air temperature above them differently?

Possible hypothesis

Unpainted metal surfaces will cause the greatest change in air temperature.

Level of difficulty

Intermediate

Approximate cost of materials

£3.00

Materials needed

» Access to several outdoor surfaces that are parallel to the ground, such as tarmac, concrete, plastic, wood, metal, soil, grass, and sand. Note: Be careful with metal surfaces in the sun – they get very hot.

» A bucket or paddling pool, and water

» Alcohol thermometers, one for each surface you will test

» Bubble wrap

» Two elastic bands

» A watch or stopwatch

Here is a book and a website you could start with in your research:

» *Matter and Energy: Principles of Matter and Thermodynamics*, Paul Fleisher (Lerner Publishing Group, 2002)

» Starchild: The sun: http://starchild.gsfc.nasa.gov/docs/StarChild/solar_system_level2/sun.html

Outline of methods

1. Locate the outdoor surfaces you will use for the experiment. They should be close together so you can easily check the temperature at each area during the course of the experiment. A playground or a garden might be a good location. Be sure that the places you choose will stay sunny during the two-hour time period you'll need for the experiment. You should include at least five different surfaces for your tests.

Continued

2. One surface to test is water. It is safest to use a bucket or a paddling pool filled with water. You are testing the air temperature at the surface, so you need to create one thermometer that floats in water. Do this by attaching a strip of thin bubble wrap on the back of one thermometer using two elastic bands. Before doing your experiment test the thermometer to make sure it floats at the surface of the water.

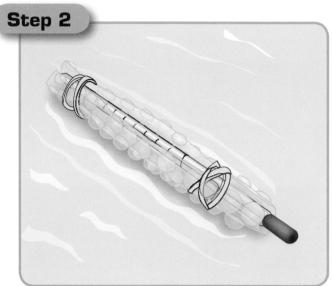

Step 2

3. Put all of the thermometers on a flat surface indoors for five minutes. They should all register the same temperature.

Step 4

4. Place a thermometer on each of your outdoor surfaces. Record the temperature at each location.

5. Observe and record the temperature at each location every 10 minutes for two hours.

6. Repeat the procedure on two other days with similar weather conditions.

7. Graph your results for each day and compare them.

Analysis of results

» Above which surface was the air temperature the highest? Above which was the air temperature the lowest?

» If you started your experiment early in the day, did the air above any surface take a longer time to reach the same temperature as the air above another surface?

» What factors, such as the colour of the surfaces or the air flow over the surfaces, do you think had an effect on the temperature?

More activities to extend your investigation

» Increase the total amount of time during which you record the temperature changes; increase the duration of the intervals as well. For example, record the temperature every 30 minutes for eight hours.

» Include additional surfaces in your experiment.

» Research the composition of each material you tested.

» Extend the recording through the evening to determine which location loses heat most quickly.

» Try the experiment at different times of the day and compare the results.

Project extras

» Show your data in both table and graph forms.

» Include photographs of each location you tested.

» Graphically display your results using thermometers copied onto paper. Colour the centre of each thermometer to the highest temperature you measured in each location.

A sound solution

Sound waves are a form of energy that can be a great source of entertainment. Unfortunately, one person's music is another's noise pollution. Headphones are a good way to direct sound waves directly to your ears, insulating the sound from everyone else. But what other materials act as sound **insulators?** In this experiment, you will test different bubble wraps to find out whether they are effective sound insulators.

Do your research

You'll need a recording with sound on it for this experiment. Your favourite music will work, but it would be better to record about two minutes of a single sound, such as the beep from a smoke detector or the note from an electric keyboard. Before you begin this project, do some research on sound and sound waves. Once you've done some research, you can tackle this project. Or, you may come up with your own unique project after you've read and learned more about the topic.

Here are some books and websites you could start with in your research:

» *The Science of Sound: Projects and Experiments with Music and Sound Waves*, Steve Parker (Heinemann, 2005)

» *Science Files: Light and Sound*, Chris Oxlade (Hodder Wayland, 2005)

» Hearing and sound: http://library.advanced.org/19537/

Background information

Possible question

Does the size of the air bubbles in bubble wrap affect how well they absorb sound energy?

Possible hypothesis

Bubble wrap with smaller air bubbles will absorb sound energy better.

Level of difficulty

Intermediate

Approximate cost of materials

£20.00

Materials needed

» A sound source, such as a small battery-operated tape recorder or an mp3 player with speakers
» A cassette tape or similar with a sound of constant volume on it
» Fresh batteries
» Clear sticky tape
» A long indoor space
» A tape measure
» Sheet of large-bubble bubble wrap
» Sheet of medium-bubble bubble wrap
» Sheet of small-bubble bubble wrap
» Small corrugated-cardboard box
» A **decibel** meter (optional)

» Physical properties of sound: http://www.cartage.org.lb/en/themes/sciences/Physics/Acoustics/PropertiesSound/PropertiesSound.htm
» What is sound?: http://www.bbc.co.uk/schools/ks3bitesize/science/physics/sound_1.shtml
» How hearing works: http://health.howstuffworks.com/hearing.htm

Outline of methods

1. Put your recorded sound and fresh batteries into your sound source recorder. Turn the volume to a low-to-medium setting. Tape the volume control in place so it will not change volume as you cover it with bubble wrap.

2. Place the recorder on the floor of your chosen indoor space. Use tape to mark the placement of the recorder so you can return it to the same place for each trial of the experiment. Turn on the recorder and listen to the volume of the sound.

Continued

3. Move away from the recorder until the sound is very faint or until you can't hear it at all. Measure and record the distance between you and the recorder. This is your control. If you have access to a decibel meter, you can record the decibel level for each trial at the same distance from the recorder.

4. Create three bubble wrap envelopes for the recorder so you can slide it in quickly after you turn it on. Be consistent in the way that you cut and tape the wrap to make the envelopes. Tightly seal the joins. Leave one flap of each envelope open until you are ready to use it.

Step 5

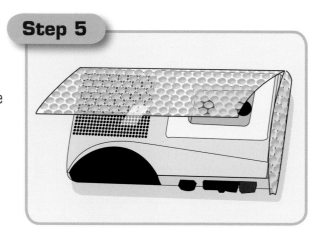

5. Rewind the recording and turn on the recorder. Slip the recorder into the large-bubble bubble wrap and seal the opening. Walk away from the recorder as you did before, until the sound is very faint or until you can't hear it at all. Measure and record the distance.

6. Carefully remove the recorder from the bubble wrap and turn it off.

7. Repeat steps 5 and 6 with the two remaining bubble wrap envelopes.

Step 8

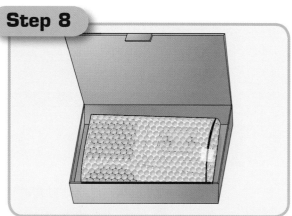

8. Repeat steps 5 to 7, but this time cover the recorder with the cardboard box as well as wrapping it in bubble wrap for each trial.

9. Repeat the entire experiment at least two more times. Average your results. To take an average, add the distances for each type of bubble wrap; then divide this number by the number of trials.

Analysis of results

» Did the bubble wrap cause the sound levels to decrease?

» Did the size of the bubbles affect the distance at which the sound became very faint or inaudible?

» How did covering the recorder with the box affect the sound levels?

More activities to extend your investigation

» Try other materials to soundproof the recorder, such as egg cartons or papers of different thicknesses.

» Research the materials used to soundproof a recording studio.

» Research decibels and how a decibel meter is used.

Project extras

» Show your results in both table and chart forms.

» Make a diagram of the place in which you carried out the experiment. For each trial, indicate the spot at which you ended.

» Include photos of the way you covered the sound source recorder.

» Include small pieces of each type of bubble wrap.

Raising static

Static electricity causes a number of different reactions. It can cause paper to stick to a comb; it might give you a shock when you reach for a doorknob; and it can even mess up your hair when you pull on a jumper. How strong can it get? Do some materials create more static electricity than others? Try this electrifying experiment to find out more about it.

Do your research

Static electricity is created by a loss or gain of electrons in certain materials. It is easiest to create in cool, dry environments, so you will get the best results if you do this experiment on a cold, dry day. Before you begin this project, do some research on static electricity. Once you've done some research, you can tackle this project. Or, you may come up with your own unique project after you've read and learned more about the topic.

You could start your research with this book and these websites:

» *Electricity*, Steve Parker and Laura Buller (Dorling Kindersley, 2005)

» The science of static electricity: http://www.thebakken.org/electricity/science-of-static.html

Background information

Possible question

Are some materials better than others for making static electricity?

Possible hypothesis

Some materials create more static electricity than others.

Level of difficulty

Easy

Approximate cost of materials

£6.00

Materials needed

» A small container of polystyrene balls (the kind used in beanbag chairs)
» Six identical plastic combs
» Squares of wool, cotton, and polyester material
» Plastic from a plastic supermarket shopping bag
» A piece of synthetic fur

» Static charge: http://www.bbc.co.uk/dna/h2g2/A6378744
» Creating charges with friction: http://www.regentsprep.org/Regents/physics/phys03/atribo/default.htm

Outline of methods

1. Divide the polystyrene balls into six piles of the same size.

2. Put the combs on a flat surface. Handle the balls and combs as little as possible to prevent you from creating static electricity before you begin your experiment.

3. Pick up one comb without touching the comb's prongs. Touch the prongs to the first pile of balls.

4. Lift the comb up and move it away from the pile. Wipe your hand across the comb to remove any balls. Count and record the number of balls picked up by the comb. This part of the experiment is the control.

Continued

5. You'll be rubbing the three squares of material, the plastic, and the piece of fur along the combs during the experiment. Decide on a method that will be consistent in each trial. For example, you might rub the materials backwards and forwards along the comb for 10 seconds, or you might rub the comb 20 times.

6. Pick up the second comb and the square of cotton material, and rub the material along the comb in the way you've decided to use in this experiment.

Step 6

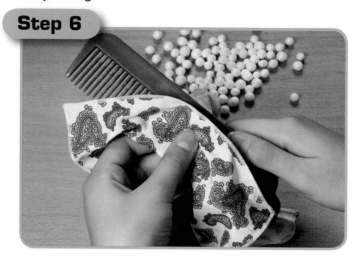

7. Touch the prongs of the comb to the second pile of balls, then lift it away from the pile as you did with the control. Count and record the number of balls picked up by the comb.

8. Repeat steps 6 and 7 using the remaining combs, materials, and piles of balls.

9. Repeat the entire experiment on two other cool, dry days and average your results. To take an average, add the number of balls recorded with each type of material; then divide the answer by the number of trials.

Step 7

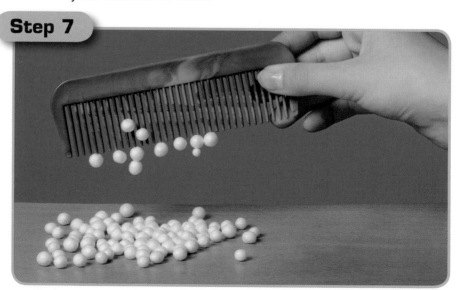

Analysis of results

» Did all the combs pick up balls?

» Were the results similar on each day you did the experiment? Were the weather conditions the same on each day?

» Did one material increase the number of balls the comb picked up? If so, which material was it?

More activities to extend your investigation

» Include research on the **triboelectric** series, a list which ranks how easily materials gain or lose electrons to create static electricity.

» Use additional materials and combs in your experiment.

» Include suggestions for other ways you would extend your experiment if you were to do it again. For example, what would happen if you used combs made of metal instead of plastic?

Project extras

» Show your results in both table and chart forms.

» Include photos of the combs with beads attached to them.

» Include samples of the materials and a sample of the polystyrene balls you used in your experiment.

Writing your report

In many ways, writing the report of your investigation is the hardest part. You've researched the science involved, and you've had fun gathering all your evidence together. Now you have to explain what it's all about.

You are the expert

Very few other people, if any, will have done your investigation. So you are the expert here. You need to explain your ideas clearly. Scientists get their most important investigations published in a scientific magazine or journal. They may also stand up at meetings and tell other scientists what they have found. Or they may display a large poster to explain their investigation. You might consider giving a talk or making a poster about your investigation, too. But however scientists present their investigations, they always write it down first – and you must too. Here are some tips about what you should include in your report.

Some hints for collecting your results

» **Making a table:** Tables are great for recording lots of results. Use a pencil and ruler to draw your table lines, or make a table using a word processing program. Put the units (m, s, kg, N and so on) in the headings only. Don't write them into the main body of your table. Try to make your table fit one side of paper. If you need two sheets of paper, make sure you write the column headings on the second sheet as well.

» **Recording your results:** It is often easy to forget to write down your results as they come in. Or you might just scribble them onto the back of your hand, and then wash your hands! A wise scientist will always make a neat, blank table in their lab book before starting. They will write down their results as they go along and not later on.

» **Odd stuff:** If something goes wrong, make a note of it. This will remind you which results might not be reliable.

» **Precision:** Always record your readings to the precision of your measuring equipment. For example, if you have scales that show 24.6 g, don't write 24 or 25 in your table. Instead, write 24.6 because that's the precise measurement.

Laying out your report

You could use the following headings to organise your report in a clear manner:

» **A title**
This gives an idea of what your investigation is about.

» **Aims**
Write a brief outline of what you were trying to do. It should include the question you were trying to answer.

» **Hypothesis**
This is your scientific prediction of what will happen in your investigation. Include notes from your research to explain why you think your prediction will work out. It might help to write it out as: "I think … will happen because …"

» **Materials**
List the equipment you used to carry out your experiments. Also say what any measuring equipment was for. For example, "scales (to weigh the objects)".

» **Methods**
Explain what you actually did in your investigation.

» **Results**
Record your results, readings, and observations clearly.

» **Conclusions**
Explain how closely your results fitted your hypothesis. You can find out more about this on the next page.

» **Bibliography**
List the books, articles, websites or other resources you used in your research.

And finally ... the conclusions

There are two main bits to your conclusions. These are the "Analysis" and the "Evaluation". In the analysis you explain what your evidence shows, and how it supports or disproves your hypothesis. In the evaluation, you discuss the quality of your results and their reliability, and how successful your methods were.

Your analysis

You need to study your evidence to see if there is a relationship between the variables in your investigation. This can be difficult to spot in a table, so it is a good idea to draw a graph. You should always put the dependent variable on the vertical axis, and the independent variable on the horizontal axis. The type of graph you need to draw depends on the type of variables involved:

» A bar chart if the results are **categoric**, such as hot/cold, male/female.
» A line graph or a scattergram if both variables are **continuous**, such as time, length, or mass.

Remember to label the axes to say what each one shows, and the unit used. For example, "time in s" or "height in cm". Draw a line or curve of best fit if you can.

Explain what your graph shows. Remember that the reader needs help from you to understand your investigation. Even if you have spotted a pattern, don't assume that your reader has. Tell them. For example, "My graph shows that the more salt used, the lower the freezing point". Circle any points on your graph that seem anomalous (too high or too low).

Your evaluation

Did your investigation go well, or did it go badly? Was your evidence good enough for you to support or disprove your hypothesis? Sometimes it can be difficult for you to answer these questions. But it is really important that you try. Scientists always look back at their investigations. They want to know if they could improve their methods next time. They also want to know if their evidence is reliable and valid. Reliable evidence can be repeated with pretty much the same results. Valid evidence is reliable, and it should answer the question you asked in the first place. As before, remember that you are the person who knows your investigation the best. Don't be afraid to show off valid evidence. And be honest if it's not!

Glossary

accurate close to the true value

alloy mixture of two or more metals

categoric variable that can be given labels, such as male/female

circuit path that an electric current follows

conductivity ability of a material to transfer heat or electricity

conductor material that is able to transfer heat or electricity

continuous variable that can have any value, such as weight or length

control something that is left unchanged in order to compare results against it

data factual information

D battery type of battery

decibel unit of measurement of the volume of sound

electrode solid conductor used in an electrolyte solution

electrolyte solution through which electric current flows

electromagnet magnet created with electricity

evidence data that has been checked to see if it is valid

gauge measurement of wire thickness

hypothesis scientific idea about how something works, before the idea has been tested

incandescent glowing with light when heated

insulator material that does not allow energy to pass through

lumen unit of measurement of the brightness of light

prediction say in advance what you think will happen, based on scientific study

solution mixture that consists of two or more substances

triboelectric to do with electricity that is produced by friction

variable something that can change; is not set or fixed

wattage measure of the amount of electric power

Index

air temperature, 32–35

background information
air temperature, 33
coloured light, 9
conduction, 21
electrolytes, 17
electromagnets, 25
incandescent light, 29
magnet temperature, 13
sound insulation, 37
static electricity, 41
bibliographies, 45
books, 4, 8, 12, 16, 20, 24, 29, 33, 36–37, 40

clothing, 44
coloured light, 8–11
conclusions, 45, 46
conduction, 20–23
control groups, 6

dependent variables, 6, 46

electrolytes, 16–19
electromagnets, 24–27

final report, 44–45

hypotheses
air temperature, 33
coloured light, 9
conduction, 21
display of, 44
electrolytes, 17
electromagnets, 25
final report and, 45
formation of, 5, 6, 7
incandescent light, 29
magnet temperature, 13
sound insulation, 37
static electricity, 41

incandescent light, 28–31
independent variables, 6, 46
Internet 4, 5

magnet temperature, 12–15
materials
air temperature, 33
coloured light, 9
conduction, 21
electrolytes, 17
electromagnets, 25
final report and, 45
incandescent light, 29
magnet temperature, 13

sound insulation, 37
static electricity, 41

notes, 7

observations, 45

project journals, 7, 46

research, 4, 5, 8, 12, 15, 16, 18, 20–21, 23, 24, 27, 28–29, 31, 32–33, 35, 36–37, 39, 40–41, 43, 45
research journals, 7, 45, 46
results
air temperature, 33
coloured light, 9
conduction, 21
electrolytes, 17
electromagnets, 25
incandescent light, 29
magnet temperature, 13
rules, 6
sound insulation, 37
static electricity , 41

scientific predictions, 7

scientific questions, 4, 5
sound insulation, 36–39
static electricity, 40–43

variables, 6, 7, 46

websites, 4–5, 8, 12, 16, 20–21, 24, 29, 33, 36–37, 40–41